WITHDRAWN

Simple and Compound Sentences

Kara Murray

PowerKiDS
press

New York

Published in 2014 by The Rosen Publishing Group, Inc.
29 East 21st Street, New York, NY 10010

First Edition

Editor: Amelie von Zumbusch
Book Design: Colleen Bialecki

Photo Credits: Cover Mike Powell/Lifesize/Getty Images; p. 5 Pete Saloutos/Shutterstock.com; p. 6 Jaren Jai Wicklund/Shutterstock.com; p. 7 Vlad Ageshin/Shutterstock.com; pp. 9, 17 Stockbyte/Thinkstock; p. 11 Michaeljung/Shutterstock.com; p. 13 joSon/Iconica/Getty Images; p. 14 Deviant/Shutterstock.com; p. 15 Anton Balazh/Shutterstock.com; p. 16 Martin Poole/Digital Vision/Thinkstock; p. 18 auremar/Shutterstock.com; p. 19 iStockphoto/Thinkstock; p. 21 Golden Pixels LLC/Shutterstock.com.

Library of Congress Cataloging-in-Publication Data

Murray, Kara.
 Simple and compound sentences / By Kara Murray. — First Edition.
     pages cm. — (Core Language Skills)
 Includes index.
 ISBN 978-1-4777-0802-6 (library binding) — ISBN 978-1-4777-0977-1 (pbk.) —
 ISBN 978-1-4777-0979-5 (6-pack)
 1. English language—Sentences—Juvenile literature. 2. English language—Composition and exercises—Juvenile literature. 3. Language arts (Elementary) I. Title.
 PE1441.M87 2014
 428.2—dc23

                                        2012048595

Manufactured in the United States of America

CPSIA Compliance Information: Batch #S13PK5: For Further Information contact Rosen Publishing, New York, New York at 1-800-237-9932

Contents

The Long and Short of It

Not all sentences are the same. The two main kinds of sentences are simple and compound sentences. Simple sentences express complete thoughts. They have **subjects** and **verbs**. Consider the sentence "Carrie likes to draw." "Carrie" is the subject. The verb is "likes."

A compound sentence is one that could be split up into two simple sentences. Its parts are joined by a **conjunction**. One example is "Carrie likes to draw, and she loves her art class."

Mixing sentence types makes writing more interesting. Too many simple sentences can make writing choppy. Compound sentences express more, but their greater length can make them harder to read.

FIGURE IT OUT

What kind of sentence is this?

Isabelle can come to my party.

(See answers on p. 22)

5

Simple sentences are also called independent **clauses**. A clause is a group of words that has a subject and a verb. Independent clauses are ones that can stand on their own. Compound sentences have two independent clauses. Take the compound sentence "I was tired, but I did not fall asleep." In it, "I was tired" and "I did not fall asleep" are both independent clauses.

The name "after the ball" and a
phrase to "The dog ran after the ball."

Sentences can also have **phrases**. Phrases give extra information about the action in the sentence. The words "in the afternoon" are a phrase in the sentence "I went to Daniel's house in the afternoon."

FIGURE IT OUT

Can you identify the independent clauses in the following sentence?

Brian usually walks to school, but he likes to ride his bike.

(See answers on p. 22)

7

Many Ways to Say It

Sentences can express several kinds of thoughts. A statement expresses a fact or opinion. This kind of sentence ends in a period. An example is "David made cookies." Questions are sentences that end in question marks. "Does Elena like chocolate cake?" is a question.

An **exclamation** is a sentence that expresses strong feeling. An exclamation takes an exclamation point.

Chart of Punctuation Symbols and Their Uses

Name	Symbol	Used to End
Period	.	Statements and commands
Question mark	?	Questions
Exclamation point	!	Exclamations and commands

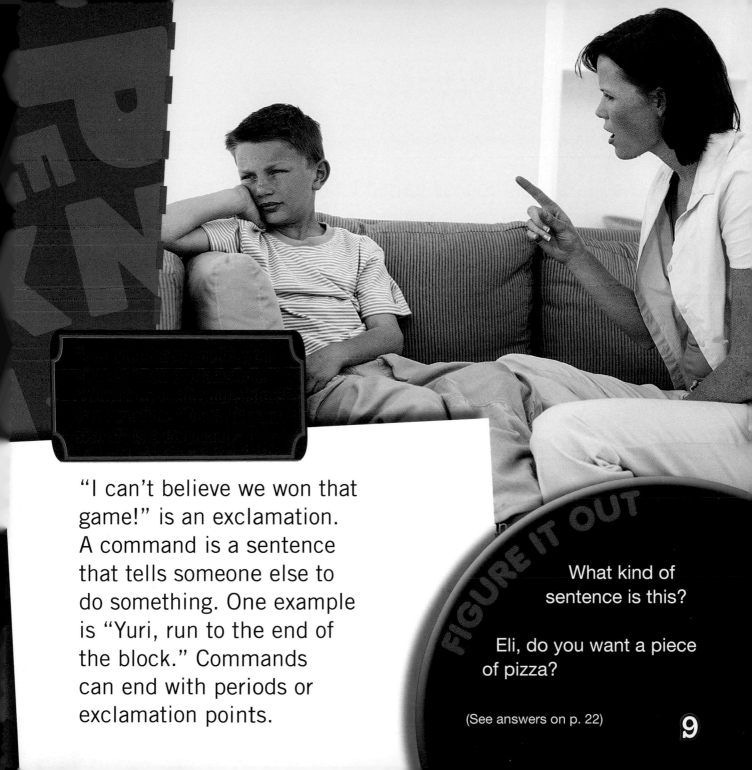

"I can't believe we won that game!" is an exclamation. A command is a sentence that tells someone else to do something. One example is "Yuri, run to the end of the block." Commands can end with periods or exclamation points.

FIGURE IT OUT

What kind of sentence is this?

Eli, do you want a piece of pizza?

(See answers on p. 22)

9

Two into One

Two simple sentences joined together with a conjunction make a compound sentence. A conjunction is a joining word. Its only purpose is to join other words together. The most important conjunction when talking about compound sentences is "and."

To make a compound sentence out of two simple sentences, you simply put a comma and the word "and" between them. For example, let's say you want to join these two simple sentences into a compound sentence: "The beach was beautiful. I wanted to stay all day." To do so, you would write, "The beach was beautiful, and I wanted to stay all day."

FIGURE IT OUT

How would
you make these
simple sentences into
one compound sentence?

Maria was late for school.
She got in trouble.

(See answers on p. 22)

The Other Conjunctions

The other conjunctions used to make compound sentences are "but," "or," "yet," "for," "nor," and "so." They all have different meanings.

"But" is used to show two facts that clash with one another. An example is the sentence "Terry wants to go to camp, but he lost the form." "Yet" is used in much the same way as "but." "Or" is used to show two possibilities. For example, "You can take the test now, or you can write a paper next week." "For" joins two connected ideas. "Nor" is used to join two negative ideas. "So" is used to show how one thought follows another.

FIGURE IT OUT

What would be the best conjunction to use to join the following two sentences?

We could have chicken for dinner tonight. We could also have hamburgers.

(See answers on p. 22)

13

All About Commas

Commas have many, many uses in sentences. In this chapter, we'll focus on a few uses in compound and simple sentences. You already know that a comma is used, along with a conjunction, to join two sentences into a compound sentence.

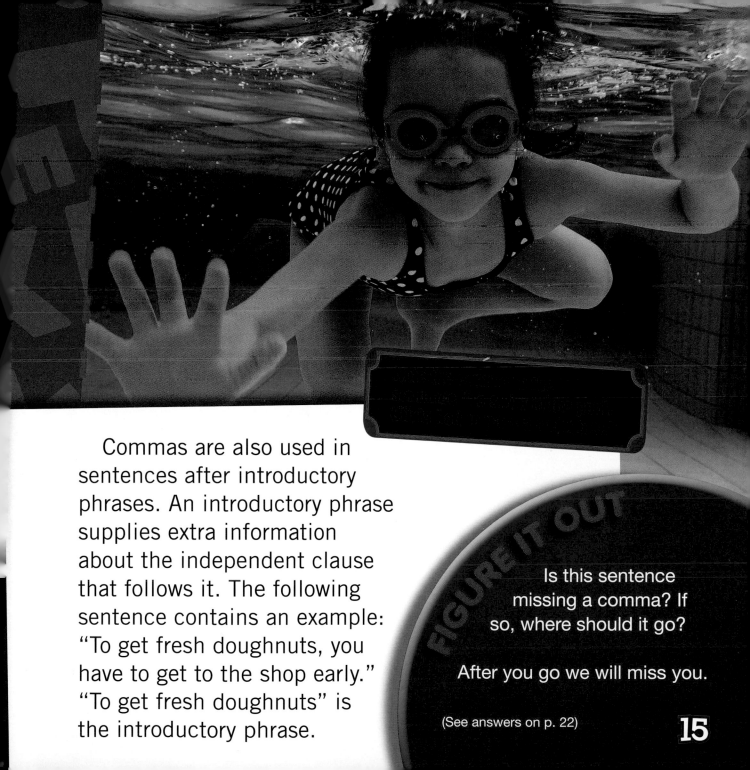

Commas are also used in sentences after introductory phrases. An introductory phrase supplies extra information about the independent clause that follows it. The following sentence contains an example: "To get fresh doughnuts, you have to get to the shop early." "To get fresh doughnuts" is the introductory phrase.

FIGURE IT OUT

Is this sentence missing a comma? If so, where should it go?

After you go we will miss you.

(See answers on p. 22)

15

The Little Words

You may be wondering about the purpose of the little words that appear in almost every sentence. Some of these little words are **determiners**. They are words that always go in front of **nouns**. They tell us specifically which noun we are talking about. For example, "the" and "my" are both determiners in the sentence "The cat scratched my brother." They tell us which cat and which brother.

The words "a," "an," and "the" are determiners. The determiners in the following sentence are "the," "an," and "the."

Some determiners are **articles**, such as "a," "an," and "the." Some are **possessives** or possessive nouns. Determiners can be numbers, too. They can also be **pronouns**, such as "each," "those," "some," "both," or "that."

FIGURE IT OUT

Can you identify the determiner in the following sentence?

Those apples are delicious.

(See answers on p. 22)

17

Relationship Words

Prepositions are words that describe the relationship that nouns and pronouns have to other words in a sentence. Think of the many ways you might describe someone's position in relation to a chair. Someone could sit on the chair, in the chair, on top of the chair, under the chair, or next to the chair. "On," "in," "on top of," "under," and "next to" are all prepositions.

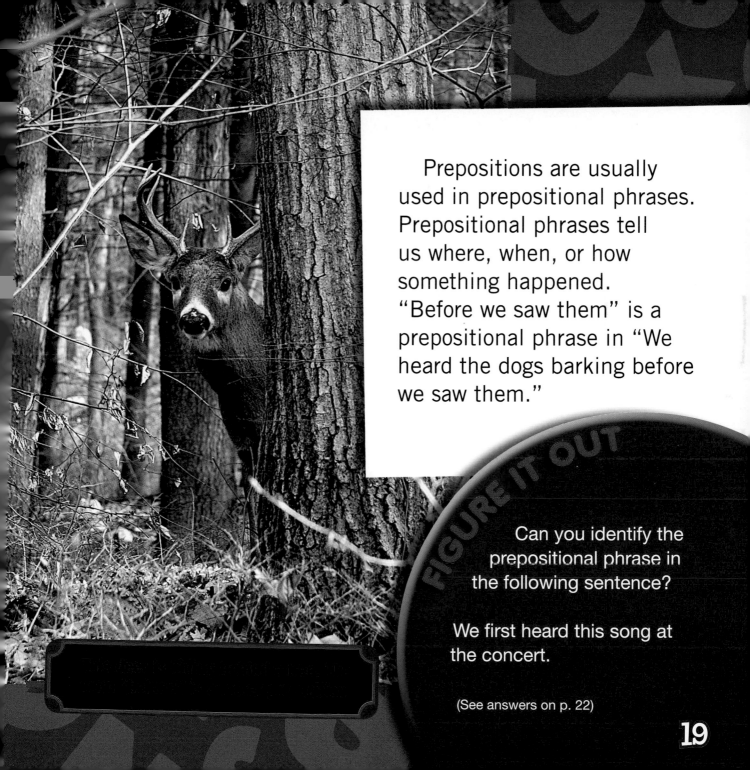

Prepositions are usually used in prepositional phrases. Prepositional phrases tell us where, when, or how something happened. "Before we saw them" is a prepositional phrase in "We heard the dogs barking before we saw them."

FIGURE IT OUT

Can you identify the prepositional phrase in the following sentence?

We first heard this song at the concert.

(See answers on p. 22)

19

Mixing Things Around

Sentences are flexible. You can take away parts, add them, or move them around. Each will make your reader take away something different in reading.

For example, let's take the simple sentence "I hope to go to Hawaii for my vacation." You could add an **adverb** and say, "I really hope to go to Hawaii for my vacation." You could make a compound sentence by adding an independent clause. For example: "I hope to go to Hawaii for my vacation, and I might stay with my friends who live there." Rewriting and moving things helps writers express exactly what they want to say.

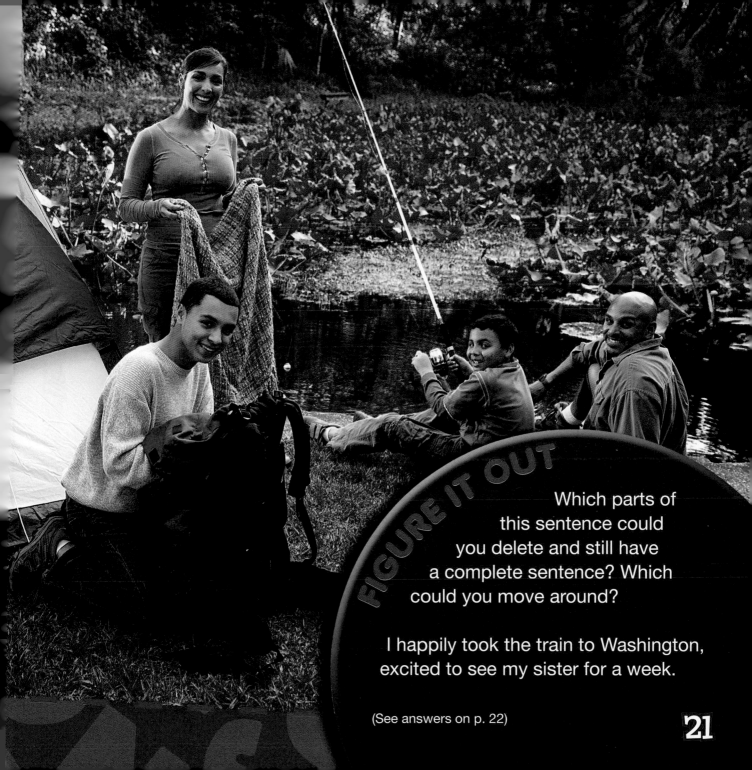

FIGURE IT OUT

Which parts of this sentence could you delete and still have a complete sentence? Which could you move around?

I happily took the train to Washington, excited to see my sister for a week.

(See answers on p. 22)

Figure It Out: The Answers

Page 5: It is a simple sentence.

Page 7: "Brian usually walks to school" is an independent clause. "He likes to ride his bike" is also an independent clause.

Page 9: It is a question.

Page 11: You would write, "Maria was late for school, and she got in in trouble."

Page 13: The best conjunction would be "or." Having chicken for dinner is one possibility. Having hamburgers is another possibility.

Page 15: It is missing a comma. It should read, "After you go, we will miss you."

Page 17: The determiner in the sentence is "those."

Page 19: The prepositional phrase is "at the concert."

Page 21: The basic element of this sentence is "I took the train." Therefore, you could delete "happily," "to Washington," and "excited to see my sister for a week." You could move the phrase "excited to see my sister for a week" to the beginning of the sentence. A comma should then follow it.

Glossary

adverb (AD-verb) A word that describes a verb, adjective, or another adverb.

articles (AR-tih-kulz) Words such as "a," "an," and "the," which are used with nouns to make their meaning clearer.

clauses (KLAWZ-ez) A group of words that includes a subject and a verb.

conjunction (kun-JUNK-shun) A word that joins two phrases or clauses together.

determiners (dih-TER-min-erz) Words or groups of words that introduce nouns.

exclamation (eks-kluh-MAY-shun) Words that express strong feeling.

nouns (NOWNZ) People, places, ideas, states, or things.

phrases (FRAYZ-ez) Groups of words that have meaning but are missing subjects or verbs.

possessives (puh-ZEH-sivz) Words that show having or ownership.

prepositions (preh-puh-ZIH-shunz) Words that explain the relationship between nouns or pronouns and other words.

pronouns (PRO-nowns) Words that can take the place of nouns.

subjects (SUB-jektz) Nouns or pronouns that carry out the action in a sentence.

verbs (VERBZ) Words that describe actions.

Index

Websites

Due to the changing nature of Internet links, PowerKids Press has developed an online list of websites related to the subject of this book. This site is updated regularly. Please use this link to access the list:

www.powerkidslinks.com/cls/sent/